ROGUE

READER

Current poetry by:
Jason Goodman

What is all wisdom
save a collection
of platitudes?

— Norman Douglas

Additional books by Jason Goodman:

Blood on My Hands and a Knife in My Back

Simple Reflections on a Frozen Surface

Nervous Reader

Nervous Reader/Second Edition

a. PUZZLED EXISTENCE

Urban Gothic

Urban Gothic 2

The Chronicles of Pain

Rogue Reader

Inquiries:
Alchemy Studio, Inc. Art & Design
Fine Literary works
Lititz, Pennsylvania, and Westport, Ireland
www.alchemystudioinc.com

Frank W. Kresen
PROOF POSITIVE
Copy Editing/Proofreading
www.artisankimwalsh.com

Joshua Riggan
Graphic Design Studios
Jriggan123@gmail

Interior Layout Design:
Kimberly Walsh
Artisan Graphic Design
www.artisankimwalsh.com

Printed in the United States of America

x

ACKNOWLEDGMENTS

Front-cover design
Alchemy Studio, Inc.

Back-cover photograph
Teresa Fee/Goodman

Illustrations: Pages 21, 23, 37, 40, 66, 105, 115
Jason Goodman

Illustrations: Pages 82, 139
Teresa Fee/Goodman

INTRODUCTION

Sometime during the single-digit period of my life, I began to write poetry. Why poetry? you may ask. I think the answer to that question can be found in the pages of an early edition of *Reader's Digest*. My childhood was spent in a cold, gray coal town located in Northeastern Pennsylvania. I knew at an early age that I would have to abandon the town of my birth, and, in preparation, I started to read things like *Word Power Made Easy* and *Vocabulary for the Age*s. In pursuit of an adequate understanding of the English language, I stumbled upon poetry and its close relative, prose. My diligence paid off handsomely. My first book of poetry, *SIMPLE REFLECTIONS ... on a frozen surface*, was published in 1972, and the rest just followed. In those early days, I used to read my work in front of a live audience. Back in the '60s, you could find obscure coffeehouses, brimming with the scent of cigarettes and coffee, where an occasional open-mic night added some cultural ambience to the room. Over the years, I read in Manhattan, with the New York Poetry Society, and San Francisco, at the City Lights Bookstore. While living in Boulder, Colorado, I met Allen Ginsberg and read by invitation at Colorado State University. Ginsberg and I shared a stage and microphone on that occasion. Another literary luminary of the time, Archibald MacLeish, told me at King's University in Wilkes-Barre, Pennsylvania, that he really enjoyed my work. He said that it made him laugh.

Poetry has been an integral part of my life, something that has always been there, providing a schematic from which a portion of life could be constructed. Poetry is a means to translating a difficult end—it can illustrate love when other words fail, define empathy in simple language, and make some of life's complexity negotiable. What you hold in your hands is a compilation of my most recent work. Here is a volume of verse which addresses our world today, verse which attempts to add to the understanding of society in the 21st century. Allow me to open a window and make the atmosphere of modern life more breathable.

DEDICATION

It never fails to amaze me
how sustainable Teresa's love is.
Every day I must remind myself
how fortunate I really am to have been
chosen by this woman.

ROGUE READER

The black candle burned
with the intensity
of twilight.
Somewhere in the distance,
water dripped.
After close examination,
it turned out to be my eyes.
Can I educate
my subconscious to see the light?
Will my sight
penetrate this night?
"Nay," I hear said
from that same voice
speaking in my head,
a voice I know well.
Going by the accent,
it originates in hell!

Will our thoughts
ever converge
when we move the vanishing
point
on a regular basis?
Our parallel thinking
is doomed to never meet,
two minds in harmony,
unaware
of the other's existence.
Mental perspectives,
lines of thought
that appear to meet,
though that convergence
was never meant to be.

Once a match
is lighted,
and starts to really burn,
a slight breeze
will not extinguish it,
and it will light another
in turn.

"If you can't get laid,
might as well get drunk!"
George, a friend of mine,
told me that one day.
Unfortunately,
George is dead!
It was a combination
of alcoholism
and syphilis
that got him in the end.

If the women
of this world
outnumber the men,
why
am I alone
again?

Watch what you say,
for fear of telling the truth.
Be careful where you look—
those eyes could see a lie.
Don't write anything down.
Libel and defamation are
viable legal pursuits.
Be careful where you stand.
It could doom your very soul,
leaning left or right
toward eternal gloom, forever
challenged to suffer,
reliving a terminal lie,
repeating over and over again,
exhausting your account with
Satan,
leaving you

completely destitute
and naked.

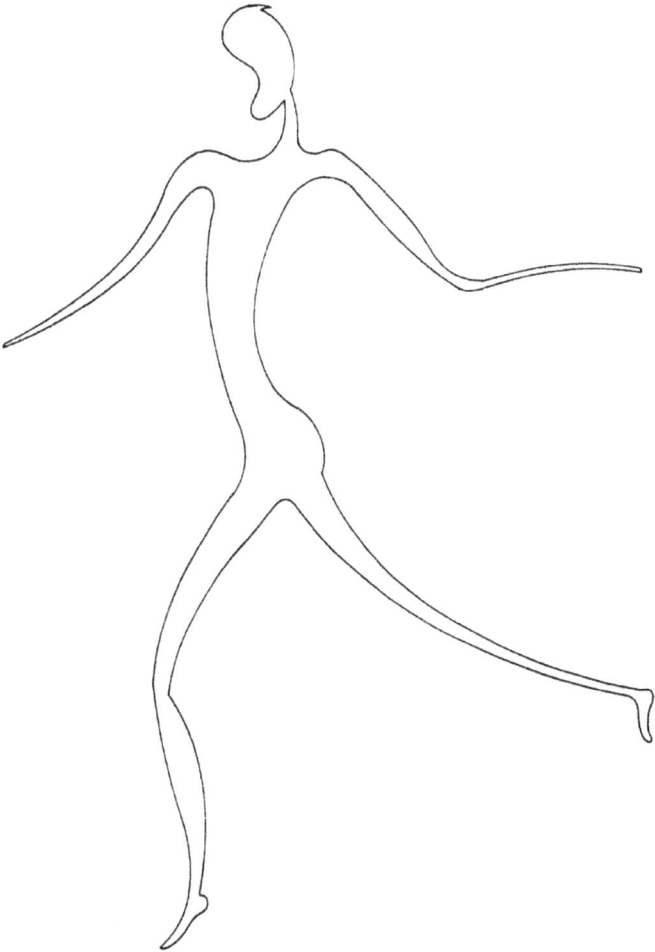

Lesbians always tell me
they are lesbian,
without my asking the
question first.
Why do I need to know?
It's not like I'm going
to make a pass,
or even ask
to go to bed with me.
Lesbians always shout
that they are lesbian.
Nobody seems to care
one way or another.
People have always loved
each other in their own
peculiar way.

ROGUE AWAKENINGS

The woman weighed in heavy.
She knew the price of pizza
but went ahead and ate it anyway.
That perfect crust
and handpicked greens.
When it comes to pizza
nothing is what it seems.
Now her weight is high,
and her husband has an eye
for a smaller bed partner.
One day he'll disappear,
having gone to work
and never returning.
If that happens,
she will order a pizza
with everything.

I had two mothers
in the barrio.
At the meeting,
the most important person
never showed up.
He could be drunk on rum
in Montego
or lying in a shallow grave
with a double tap
in his head.
You don't mess with these people.
They are experienced
at making wise guys dead.

Oh! that
brutal sickness,
reality.
A long night
of libations.
Balzac would be proud of me.
Indecent pleasures,
indistinct pursuits
under a dubious
influence.
Oh! that
pain of morning light,
hidden away conveniently
from bloodshot sight.

An outhouse
always flushed,
and the seat
is always up,
a Sears & Roebuck catalog
with the bra section
torn out.
My brothers are quick, or it
was dear dad
fondling his dick.

We are never
given enough time
to learn about life.
Our waking hours
are overwhelmed
with thoughts of strife.
Our restless nights
are given over to fear,
blatant hunger,
and the realization
we haven't a clue
what's right—
nor do we have a clue
about life.

I went and got all dressed up
just to have
the correct dream.
My old wardrobe
simply dropped me into
your personal nightmare,
and the change
was needed anyway.
My shoes were shined.
I picked out the right tie,
not the loud thing
with the naked fat lady.
I was dressed with skill.
My choices inspired
simple overkill,
just for the thrill
of having a real,

normal dream
about you.

Sweet, noxious death
scattered across the field,
its grass stained red,
unconcealed.
Blood permeating
the very topsoil,
weapons rust
without an appeal
to the once-straining arms,
slashing, swinging blades,
whistling through flesh
of our next
generation.
Youth spent, exhausted,
wasted as death congealed
on this field.
Mothers weep, and

fathers speak
of the many ways
war has lost
its nobility.

Death happens to equalize
everyone's mirth.
Death ends every debate,
eliminating all merit,
snuffing out the flame of
misplaced opinion,
removing every bit of worth.
Death clarifies priorities.
Amplifying one's perspective,
it provides a soothing balm,
something to dab on reality,
eliminating the haunting
by a ghost of nothing.
Death reminds us of amends
never made,
promises never meant
to be honored,

all of the lies we tell
to those who love us.
Death renders this apology
within the universe of silence.
We scream, and no one hears;
we die and no one mourns.
Death sits in our tomb, laughing.

In this modern world,
nothing inhibits
self-gratification.
We can have it anytime,
anywhere,
juicy and sweet,
each piece two bites,
with pulp
running down my face.
While I self-gratify,
I look around the kitchen.
There is more for me
but nothing for my wife
and kids.

WINTER ON
VANDERBILT BEACH

All of these itty-bitty women
attempting to drive
their gigantic SUVs.
Escalades, Navigators
and Armadas,
which, I believe,
went to the bottom
somewhere off the coast of
Ireland.
These tiny ladies
attempting to reverse
from the parking lot,
wheeling their Tellurides,
Aviator, and Visigoths
Then
in conversation overheard, a
common refrain will emerge

concerning the price
of a gallon of
gasoline.

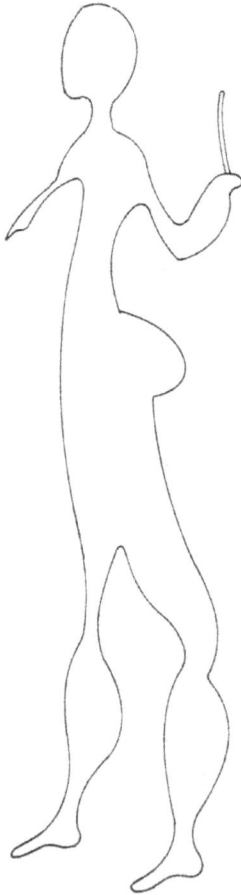

I'm just sitting here
waiting for the Viagra
to take effect.
What used to be easy
now requires
"Better Living through
Chemistry."
Just sitting around, hoping it
works this time.
My dealer assured me
that this was the real thing;
the color is blue,
the package,
sealed.
Man, what a stud!
Pneumatic pumps, injections,
and huge blue pills,

just to have a peek
at my early thrills,
or a very awkward
act of contrition.

Tired brown eyes flashed
as the whites walked by;
just enough English
understood
to realize that remark was
unkind.
Brown skin sweating,
toiling in the sun,
building another
man's empire,
with the same insults flying,
directed at krauts, gennies,
paddies, and hunkies,
exhibiting the same lack
of common decency,
not to mention
respect.

Joe's Diner

Bertie said,
"Do ya want grits
wit dat?"
I said, "Wit wat?"
She said, "Wit dat!"
So I axed her,
"How long is it gonna last?"
She said, "Wat's gonna last?"
I said, "The grits!"
She says, "Wat grits?"
I sez, "The ones wit dat!"
Bertie then sez,
"I'm glad ya axed!"
So I paid the check
and got up
and left.

Too many
aging egos
competing for
the same table.
Too many
fragile egos
trying desperately
to occupy
the same space.
"I used to do this,
I used to do that..."
Too many
aging egos
busy comparing
incontinence products
or compromised
surgical scars.

They came from Ohio,
Nebraska, Indiana,
and Illinois,
snow-white hordes
fleeing their Winter
up North.
They wait in traffic,
hoping the light will change
in their favor,
complaining about
those outta state drivers.
Somehow
the irony escapes them,
but then again, they're *ALL*
outta state drivers!
Racking up resentments
within the local residents,

many of whom
happen to live here!

The pool of water
felt like a bath
at Berkley Springs.
Her bathing costume
left very little
to my imagination.
My suntan
exposed the skin
where the ring
would have been.
I risked everything
just to prove
my age,
or youth ill spent
on frivolous things.

Platinum-colored hair,
with hours spent
on makeup,
dry, abused skin
dark brown everywhere.
If Vanderbilt
only knew
how his good name
came to be attached
to so much
caustic attitude!

Weep not for me
but for your debtors.
Shed no tears of pity and sorrow
but tears for those who borrow.
Fear not your life after death.
Soothe your fingers with jewels
and coin.
Starve any thought of charity
and nourish thoughts of envy.
Woe unto you, cursed wretch,
for someday you will grow old.
Women will turn away
and give way to death.
Wine will lose its favor
as sleep escapes your evening
endeavors.
Thank the ghost

of past behavior.
You have chosen a road of steady
decline;
you have blocked your ears
to solemn church bells' chime
and opened the portal of gluttony,
rendering the fatal blow to
autumn,
temperance, and reborn
mediocrity.
Weep again for every soul frozen
in Dante's ninth level of hell.

It never fails to amaze me
—those lofty levels
some find a need
to elevate themselves into.
It is an affront to reality,
those fathomless depths
that some individuals
knowingly submerge their
opinions through.
It is incredible
the levels to which
very small people
tend to expand
those inflatable egos,
and then argue that point and
leave,
thoroughly misunderstanding

and complaining,
begrudging
a complimentary illusion,
while cursing
another's intellect
in every conceivable way,
playing a bit part
on the stage of humanity.

CLIMATE CHANGE REALITY

Could this be hell?
The heat, humidity,
and total discomfort.
Could I have died
and not been told?
It depends upon your feelings,
emotions, temperament.
Do you feel dead?
Have you ever died before?
How would you know
if there isn't anything
to compare it to?
Is this hell?
It's so hot,
and I'm sweating profusely.
My shirt is stuck to my skin,
and I'm panting,

awash in drips
and drops of perspiration,
melting like wax
at Madame Tussaud's museum.

Day becomes night
when the black blizzards
have their way.
They plowed away the future,
leaving a bowl of dust
in their wake,
something for the children
to look forward to.
Shaking their fist at God,
blaming him in every way,
it was the drought
or maybe the wind.
It's all God's fault.
He made these fertile fields
blow away.
Now they are "next year people,"
waiting for their God to rethink

his creation,
giving them back
a measure of wheat—
expecting a blessing,
and getting a curse
instead.

Hundreds of tiny spigots
drip from my forehead and nose;
clothing becoming self-adhesive,
clinging to every pore
of my skin.
The old ones knew,
calling it *humidity*, whereas
I call it by other names
not worth repeating.
A cold shower grants a reprieve
but it's a fleeting gesture,
lasting momentarily
and increasing the misery
a hundredfold.
Those damn residents
of Mount Olympus
bestowed this fear upon me,

and I will accept a dubious gift.
But! I beg to ask the question:
Why must humidity always come
wrapped in a pre-soaked
package,
dripping from my forehead and
nose
whenever I become active?

One large eye,
fiery and unblinking,
hanging in the Eastern sky,
bloodshot and angry,
burning hapless humans
with what we call *tanning*.
We scurry from its desire
shadow to shade,
hiding, cowering,
trying to deny
that red orb its damage.

Motherfuckers
who spray "Roundup"
on the grass they mow.
Bastards.
Think of the wells and reservoirs
ruined for life,
a death as bad as running dry.
Motherfuckers,
sneaking out at night
using the cloak of darkness
to water that precious
lawn of theirs.
Selfish little bastards.
While half the world
drinks filthy water,
their kids dying
from cholera and diarrhea.

Those selfish bastards
who mow their grass at any hour,
night and day.
It doesn't really matter.
They are not concerned
as long as their lawns are green
and nicer than the neighbors'.

That green waste

They plant grass
only to watch it grow,
but the problem arises
when it's time to mow.
That carpet of green
will not feed a bee,
or satiate any bug.
It just lies there,
basically dead,
without a decent eulogy.
They plant grass
just for something to do,
every weekend spent
trying to make anew
that barren expanse

both green and dead,
infertile to most creatures,
every blade wearing
a chemical disguise.
They plant grass,
and everything else
just dies.

DYING FROM COVID-19

AUTHOR'S NOTE:

On May 25, 2020, I was infected with the COVID-19 virus. My wife drove me to the VA Medical Center in Lebanon, Pennsylvania, where I was placed on a ventilator. My blood oxygen concentration level dropped to 30%! For the next 16 days, while in a chemically induced coma, I was turned stomach to back every 8 hours. They told my wife that I was not going to make it, hinting at her plans for the disposition of my body.

Somehow, I managed to survive that ordeal, having spent a total of 28 days in hospital. My follow-up care involved an additional 5 months of pulmonary therapy.

Here are a few observations based on that experience.

For an in-depth examination of that COVID hospitalization, reference my book THE CHRONICLES OF PAIN. There is an entire chapter devoted to the COVID episode.

Jason

Fingernails
and beard growing
at an alarming rate.
All of the food
came in a bag,
never a plate.
The die has been cast.
This virus will determine
my fate.
There was a darkness.
My dreams went black.
Every eight hours
stomach to back.
They told everyone
I wasn't going to survive.
The tomb would be my home.
My dreams went black,

and no one came to greet me
at the landing
of the River Styx.

I have a spare room at home
chock full of extra prayers
of all denominations.
Using soothing words,
they have been left there
by well-intentioned people,
to help speed my recovery
from almost-certain vivid death.
I have a room right here
in this community hospital,
filled with ventilators
installed by dedicated people
trying to save my life,
or prove that they
have the power
to prolong the suffering
of my poor wife's strife.

For more than a month
I was prodded, rolled
and poked,
pleated, slapped, and shoved
basically kneaded,
a pile of ground beef
being molded and squeezed,
making little patties,
or big round balls.
As far as I knew,
my dignity was still there,
sitting patiently in the hall,
where I was told to leave it
until the day of discharge,
being returned to the herd,
or simply tossed into
a medical-waste dumpster
that is never empty.

There was a little sign
glued low on the door
way down there
with the credit card logo.
Just a few brief words—
economy of speech implied—
leave your dignity here,
by the handicap sign.
They came in and removed
my designer jeans,
the pair I paid extra for,
with a few holes
and two busted-out knees.
They handed me a gown
and said, "Put this on."
I noticed that my ass
was exposed to everyone,

flabby and sore
chilled and red.
No one seemed to care—
They had seen it all
before.

Life is very uncomfortable;
nothing seems to fit very well,
It was either too tight
or loose as hell.
I would prefer a life
designed strictly for my frame,
custom fit by some old tailor
who has a Chinese name.
Buddha and Christ
had the right idea,
sitting under a tree,
wearing nothing but a toga,
talking about love
using the word "we"
and giving our gold away.
Without any money,
the question of too many

items in the closet
tends to go away.
Nothing feels too tight
on any given day.

A bold black blunder
came intruding into my
bedchamber,
destructive little plunders
bewitching the hour of midnight.
Venture not through this darkness
if you value your life and fortune,
for the darkness will pass —
a terrible caress
taking its toll
in mental torture.
Evil is the night,
whence it completes
its sinful work
and muffles the victim's plight
with shouts of false happiness.
It creeps along the floor,

through nooks and crannies
passing,
leaving not a trace or sound
as it steals away unbound,
imitating pleasure while passing,
laughing, lying about every
detail,
rendering my emotions
bent and broken.

Tonight
my dreams will be
delivered on time —
Amazon Prime.
Something is strange.
I cannot remember
ordering any of these
things in my head.
Tonight,
my nightmares
will be delivered on time —
dark memories.
They are always the same —
sweat, fear,
and the smell of death from
my gun.

Tonight my dreams will be delivered,
compliments of Vietnam

Teresa

ROGUE WORDS

Listen,
listen—
hear that deep
bellowing noise
coming from the ground.
Is it a voice?
Is it a noise?
Is it a sound
that I must listen to?
Should I have poise
and quiet my noise,
to clarify that vibration
bellowing from the bowels
of this Earth?
Listen,
listen—
hear something

that will fill your void.
What void? you say.
Everyone has a void,
a pit that must be filled,
something said or done,
something, something terrible.
Just listen—
listen to your world
collapsing.

Misery is a peanut butter and
jelly sandwich
made without the benefit of
bread.
Misery is an upper closet door
that comes in contact with your
head.
Misery is a chain-smoker
with very rusty teeth.
Misery is a hamburger
with very little meat.
Misery is lifting weights
with a diagnosed hernia.
Misery is a piece of birthday cake
someone wrapped in a baggie.
Misery is a dentist
whose kid you beat up at school.

Misery is the teacher
who called him in the first place.
Misery is a traffic cop
when you come to a stop sign
and just pause.
Misery is following in your dad's
footsteps
only to realize that he's dead.
Misery is holding hands with a
cactus
right after your karate practice.
Misery is a surgeon
for using a blowtorch on a
patient.
Misery is removing an appendix
from a guy with a cast-iron
stomach.

Misery is watching two men in
white coats
walking up my driveway.

.

Every single day
I lock my mind away
and forget where
I put the key.
There were no bars
or visible restraints,
but
I was a prisoner
nonetheless!
Incapacitated with fear,
doomed to failure
and only to hear
the pieces of my life
shattering,
bits and pieces tinkling,
on every marble floor,
accumulating into

small piles
while clouds of dust swirl,
concealing the only door,
the portal from this reality.

The shadows of darkness
allow perversion for a while.
It stares blindly
at an illusion
of beauty.
She tells him,
Wisdom is the cure.
He is no fool—
knowing nothing
and being absolutely sure
to never learn anything—
at least those things
that matter—
like knowing how
to install a bushing,
or how to prevent
a pregnancy.

Take a hike,
you little ass wipe,
a grizzled old veteran said.
He was smoking a big cigar
at a sidewalk cafe,
when the owner of a store
asked him to move away.
The veteran said "No,"
and a small confrontation ensued.
The veteran knew courage
while the ass wipe
felt fear,
necessitating a slow retreat.
While he walked away,
the veteran smiled
and said, *Have a nice day!*

I may want you
but not love you.
I will awaken
deep in the night
and reach for you,
unfortunately, finding only
my other pillow
at my side.
I laugh and then sigh,
Why?
Why must the night
add cruelty
to indecision?

Damn those ups

taken this morning,
provoking the afternoon
to be so confusing.
I'm running around
in a daze—
nothing gentle,
nothing kind—simply a
maelstrom for the mind.

ONE

The number one
is loneliness
unless one is conceited.
The number two
is loveliness,
for in it,
one is needed.

My name is Jake.
I live inna gutter,
never knew no mudder.
My fadda was a whiskey, never
knowed no kin.
Boy! I wish I had some gin.
Me clothes is ripped and torn.
Of the whole city I'm the scorn.
Me's vocabulary is filthy
an' dirty.
Me's shoes is busted and worn.
I try to work whenever I kin.
Boy! I wish I had some gin.
Iffin' I was rich and hadda car,
you'd bet your boots itta hav ah
bar.
Iffin' I was rich and hadda
house,

you'd bet your last buck
idah have a spouse
an' a bunch of little kin.
I'd beat 'em silly
iffin I caught 'em drinkin!
Before I get rich and handsome,
and before they finish my yacht,
and before I get all of them kin—
before I wish fer alla dis
I foist gotta wish fer gin.

Opium

That meager wrath
of bloodstained clouds
rushing by from East to West
to settle an old score
dating back centuries,
humiliation
at the hands of destiny.
Or was it dynasty?
A confrontation
developing over tea—
better war technology
won the day,
though pungent memories
were inscribed
on the minds
of every Chinese.

My wife and I
have been together
a very long time.
We've reached the point
of reading one another's mind.
I have to take
Reynold's Wrap
to fabricate
an aluminum hat,
to keep my brain safe
from her mind's roving eye.
There are things in there
which deny explanation.
Thoughts occasionally wander
to other men's wives,
and if truth
were to be revealed,

my gentle wife's demeanor
would assume the dimensions
of a very
vengeful monster.

Old automobile front seats
scream lechery,
with a stain right in the middle
that won't ever go away.
It was a borrowed car, no less,
that night at the drive-in.
How was a guy to know
she was suffering from gonorrhea?
Old cars with bench seats
going fast around corners, the
centrifugal conspirator
whispering,
"Slide over, baby...."
How was a guy to know
his protection was defective?
Old cars with front seats
relate a cautionary tale:

The ones with bucket seats
and a massive console
will sometimes keep a guy
out of trouble!

Some people eat
cottage cheese
with pepper.
Others prefer jam,
large curd, small curd,
and there are those few
who never eat
cottage cheese
at all.
Free from dairy,
oats, almonds, and palm,
no cow will fulfill
their mouth,
though, naturally,
my low-fat yogurt disappears
on a regular basis—
and then they always deny

their whereabouts
when it happens.

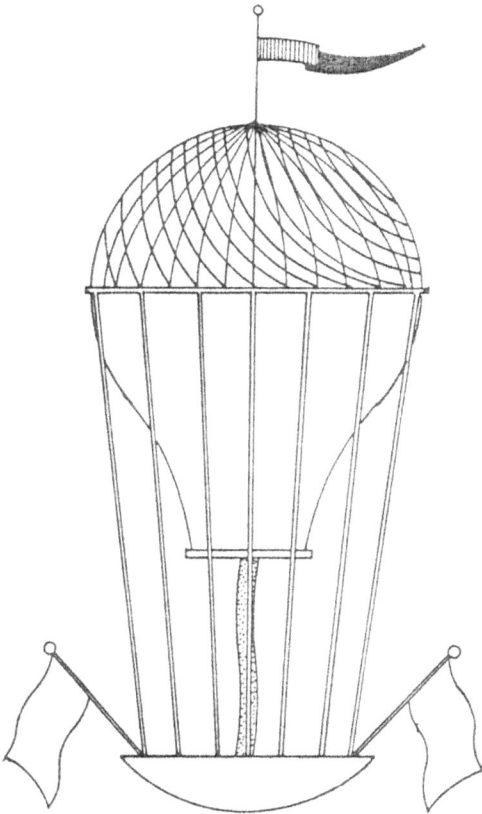

Oh! What lies
we weave into vast
webs of deceit
in our perilous quest
for petty truth.
Oh! What fibs
become these large,
hideous missteps.
Our pace quickens
toward wavering deceit.
The entire endeavor
becomes a blind
and useless
pursuit anyway.

I was once a slave,
an indentured servant,
a victim of my circumstance.
My every day
centered around acquiring
one particular substance.
I was once a slave,
indebted in every way,
ebbing on eternity
just to possess
owning a surplus
of one particular substance.
I was once a slave,
living each day
under threat of a lash,
stinging pain,
sweating sorrows,

terrified to survive
another tomorrow
without that one substance
that some simply call *love*.

One night at an AA meeting.

What actually happens
at those meetings?
Old Buicks with dents
on every corner,
sporting bumper stickers
that proclaim
a "Higher Power."
What actually occurs
at those meetings?
Always in the bowels,
down a flight of steps
into some church basement,
the smell of cheap coffee
accosting one's senses,
overheated styrofoam

and communal dementia.
What actually happens
at those meetings?
Old windbags
preaching, young men sweating
the impending
"Protection From Abuse" order.

My walls coughed up
the yellow mucus of nicotine,
while the refrigerator
entertained
a dozen cans of lager.
Everything lays askew—
dirty T-shirts and trousers
advertising a man's folly.
They say life becomes renewed
with every passing funeral
when the grim reaper
came calling,
imploring,
Come with me, oh tired soul,
gather the remnants of self.
Come with me
on that lonely path to hell.

Dedicated to my brother Mark 1948-2021

For Barbara's Paintings

The universe weeps
tears of lost galaxies,
while black holes
of nefarious origins
consume distant suns
with an unquenchable appetite.
A red dwarf, exposed
for the thief
it's been all along,
takes a leap
at the far horizon.
Someone skips a nebula
like a flat stone
on some small pond.
With every skip,

a new sun is born,
while the entire heavens
simply look on.
They have been watching
all of this happen
for many, many eons.

Hands wrenching,
teeth clenching,
anticipating
the waves of pain.
Eyes watering,
breath wringing,
anticipating
the waves of misery.
Electric pads,
iced gel packs
waiting in the freezer—
they create their own
anticipation
for when they are needed.
Frostbitten legs
and facial grimace—
bone-on-bone pain

can never be
gotten used to!

I dream
while floating
on the surface of sleep
Damn morphine—
it's always in color
and very convincing.
I awaken,
wondering
almost every time,
Did it really happen that way,
or was that real this time?

If I could only wake
from this eternal sleep
just to see the sun,
to simply stir in my bed,
and remove this dream
from my head.
Why is it necessary
for all these talking lips
to insist that I am dead
and very much gone?
If I could only wake
from this extremely dark sleep,
and have the tenacity
to keep
my eyes open

and my mind sharp—
to simply have this fog
burned from my restless brain.
If I could only wake
to prove beyond a doubt
that there is life
after death.

This frozen soul
happened in Vietnam.
You can't kill another man when
your soul has thawed.
Killing is learned behavior.
Go ahead, join the Navy—
they know how to kill another.
My soul is still frozen
in parts.
A woman's love has helped defrost
those hidden cavities,
reserved for death and lust,
rape and torture—
all of the attributes
of a trained military man.
My soul is still frozen
in many parts.

The warmth of love
has softened my heart,
though the soul
stays
extremely hard
and cold to the touch.

We accept Christ almighty
because he died on the cross,
and the people from *Reader's
Digest* saw it.
We read about him
in the Bible
and on the backs of old magazines
marked "Miscellaneous"
strewn about the laundromat.
And so secure we sit,
looking out of our bay windows,
watching our neighbors' kids
killing themselves with heroin.
Then Sunday arrives, and,
dipping from a bowl of salty
water,
we wash away our sins,

thanking some pope figure
for taking the time to bless it.
And with a passing sign,
we file in solemn ranks,
quiet and thoughtful,
while a Cadillac
with a roach-shaped hat
reads from a Stephen King book.

To forge happiness
with such crude tools—
an apathetic God,
a human race not caring.
Battling doubt
while moving mountains
with hope—for what?
A better view?
And what is self,
but a lonely
ego,
and what brings meaning
into this mental turmoil?
You, my love—you!

I raise my glass in toast
to the great departments
of disability,
for their tireless efforts
helping "my generation."
I drink long again
for all the orthopedic surgeons,
who help design
new and improved
artificial limbs.
I really slug one
for the poor family,
testing their love for "him,"
the Vietnam Veteran!

Tell me of old wives' tales,
snakebite cures,
and vagabonds
who fix pots and buy rags
on occasion.
Explain
the Big Rock Candy Mountain
Smoky Mountains,
breaking down anything
but your opinion.
Go ahead and make disgusting
noises—
armpit farting,
raspberries, and another
friction.
Go ahead and break down
anything except your well-

groomed wall
of deception!

Like a steel wedge
we spread apart
with every sledgehammer
weekend.
More precious fibers
are lost.
Separated is this love,
like a tall tree
fallen to logs.

Inlaid thoughts
of a meticulously
made mosaic,
created by an artist
not known for his
patience.
Who is Tabula
Rasa, anyway?
A back street in Athens
or an Italian prostitute?

My cigar puffs
on a rising headache,
the beer warms up
a leftover tendency, and
yet I dread the thought
of calling this *misery.*
My mind copulates with
creative things, leaving
them unsatisfied,
so I pull up my fly
only to hear the word
frustration!

Maybe I should take a trip
to hell,
to ask Faust
how he won damnation
through his contract
with Mephistopheles.
There is a distinct possibility
that Faust,
for a few gold Ducats,
will explain
how he found eternity in hell,
how he signed away
his soul,
for a woman's honor
and fine standing in heaven.

It stands to reason

accepting these bad times.

Too many yachts on the intercoastal.

Too much oceanfront construction.

Oh! it provides work for people—

men who eat a lunch

packed in a brown bag.

They are building these homes for

people who have never

had that pleasure.

My mother tells me,

this is the way of

recession!

Mercedes Benz builds cars.

Electric towel warmers

keep yacht owners happy.

Life is very comfortable

for those who own the means
of frivolous financial
servitude.

On a gray windy morning
blowing through my soul,
she threatened to leave me—
I would rather she did not go.
We have a love
as violent as
air.
Come stay with me, woman,
until the storm blows away.
On such a windy morning, my
feet crave my shoes.
They want to start walking
away from these blues.
We have a love.
Her body weight anchors mine,
holding the essence of attraction
fast above the mire.

On such a windy morning, just
choose another day
to leave me—
or simply walk away.

There is a special hell

for soldiers who kill.

They start serving their time

the moment the trigger is pulled.

Everyone thought Vietnam was

hell—little did they know

of the frozen soul

or the depth of despair that

killing another human being

would entail.

But! I was ordered

to pull that trigger

by a man of God,

who was also an officer.

Hitler's subordinates

tried that defense

at Nuremberg.

It made perfect sense—

hoping to escape

a hangman's noose,

perfectly placed

around one's neck,

assuring a clean dispatch,

an execution of merit

for crimes committed

by another man's direction.

Following orders

holds no substance

in Satan's home.

You can shout your innocence

all day long.

Afterward, you discover

walls of misery,

corridors of pain,

for sins against humanity—

it is all the same.

Dante's ninth level

is freezing cold.

Little did Dante

know

of the frozen soul!

Far down South,

down Mexico's way,
I have a friend
named Oscar,
who owns a cigar store.
Every now and then,
Oscar pulls out a few sticks
and cuts the ends.
We find a few nice chairs
and fire up the stogies —
and then proceed
to completely exaggerate
our machismo
and female conquests.

Teresa Fee Goodman

Then I found myself
in an electric oven—
maybe a microwave—

or a migraine

moment?

I think about food,

50-cent pot pies,

and money spent

on the Irish Sweepstakes.

My dreams of worry dissipate
with a slamming door,

any loud noise

within a cruel headache!

White carcass

steaming on a beach,

reeking of coconut

and leftover aftershave.

Large breasts

projecting the sun

on the twin screen

of Polaroid's identity.

May I have a glance

of your tempting ass?

Only to masturbate

with my rock glass.

INDEX OF FIRST LINES

Winter on Vanderbilt Beach

39...All of these itty-bitty women
41...I'm just sitting here
43...Tired brown eyes flashed
44...Joe's Diner
45...Too many
46...They came from Ohio,
48...The pool of water,
49...Platinum-colored hair,
50...Weep not for me
52...It never fails to amaze me

Climate Change Reality

55...Could this be hell?
57...Day becomes night
59...Hundreds of tiny spigots
61...One large eye,
62...Motherfuckers
64...They plant grass

Dying from COVID-19

Rogue Words

www.ingramcontent.com/pod-product-compliance
Lightning Source LLC
LaVergne TN
LVHW021500080426
835509LV00018B/2358